T. S. Thompson

God is Able

A Study of 2 Corinthians 9:8

Scripture taken from the King James Version is marked with (KJV) at the end of a quotation.

Scripture taken from the Christian Standard Bible is marked with (CSB) on the end of a quotation.

Butterfly Light Press, LLC

www.butterflylightpress.com

Mailing address: P.O. 2052 Westminster, Maryland 21158

Books are available at special discounts for bulk orders.

Book design and photography done by Passionate Portraits

www.passionateportraitsweb.com

A special thanks to editor David Aretha

ISBN 978-1-7327181-2-8 (paperback)

ISBN 978-1-7327181-3-5 (eBook)

Library of Congress Control Number: 2019948294

Printed in the United States of America

10 9 8 7 6 5 4 3 2 1

I dedicate this book to Rose, my dear friend and sister in Christ. Thank you for being a part of my life and encouraging me as a Christian author.

Table of Contents

2 Corinthians 9:8 (KJV)

And God is able to make all grace abound toward you;
that ye, always having all sufficiency in all things,
may abound to every good work:

Preface

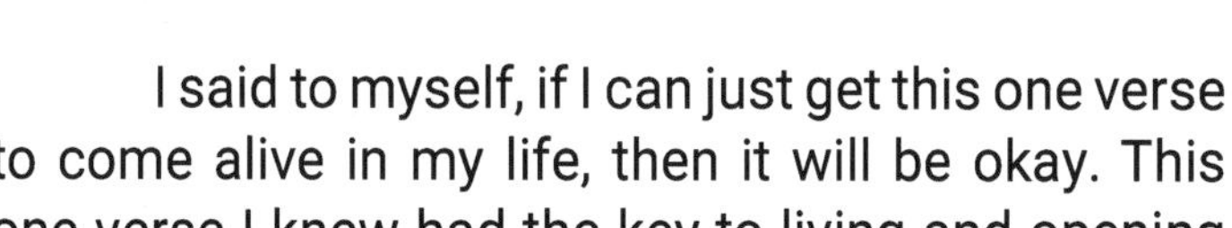

I said to myself, if I can just get this one verse to come alive in my life, then it will be okay. This one verse I knew had the key to living and opening up the promises of God.

I meditated on the verse 2 Corinthians 9:8 for two years, seeking God for understanding and marveling at the revelations on His Word He gave me. This book is an in-depth look at those revelations on that verse and how it changed how I see God and my relationship with Him.

May this book enlighten and enrich your walk with God. I hope this verse comes alive in your life so you can always have all sufficiency in all things and abound to every good work God calls you to do.

A Study of 2 Corinthians 9:8

2 Corinthians 9:8 (KJV)

And God is able to make all grace abound toward you;
that ye, always having all sufficiency in all things,
may abound to every good work:

Chapter 1: God is Able

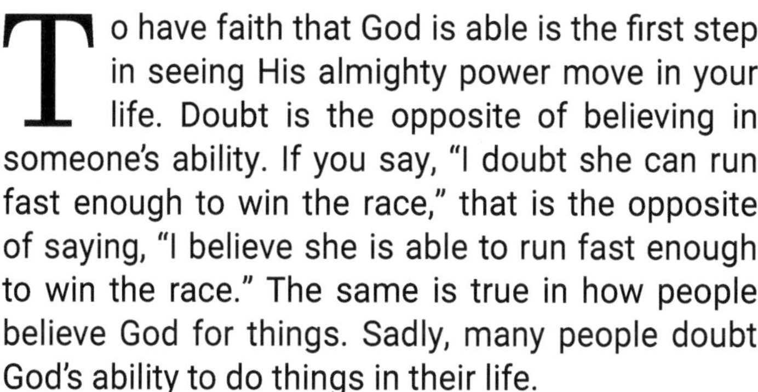

To have faith that God is able is the first step in seeing His almighty power move in your life. Doubt is the opposite of believing in someone's ability. If you say, "I doubt she can run fast enough to win the race," that is the opposite of saying, "I believe she is able to run fast enough to win the race." The same is true in how people believe God for things. Sadly, many people doubt God's ability to do things in their life.

One thing I noticed right away with this verse was that it did not say, "And God makes all..." No, it says He is *able to*. The word *able* implies it is not an automatic thing. At first I wondered if there is any reason that would keep God from being able to—or let me rephrase it: unwilling. Because if He is able, I would need to believe God is also willing.

I pondered if sin may keep God from being able to make all grace abound toward me. In the next chapter I go into more detail on grace. But I will just mention here that grace is unmerited. That is the reference to and what God is able to do: to make all His grace abound toward you. If we go even further into the verse it talks about the purpose of God's grace to abound toward you, so you will possess the means to help others. So I do not see God withholding His grace to prevent us from having what we need to assist and bless others. That sounds absurd.

With that answered for me, I came to the part of needing to believe He was also willing—not just able to, but willing. Admittedly I struggled with this part for a good deal of time. I believed God was able, that He had the power to act, and I trusted in the promises of His word. So it was never about doubting God's ability.

There are plenty of people in this world able to do things or help, but they choose not to. There are also people willing to help, yet cannot. However, God is above people. I look to God for what He is capable of and not base it off of past disappointments in others. Therefore, I went to the Word for other scriptures of God being willing.

3 John 2 (KJV)

Beloved, I wish above all things that
thou mayest prosper
and be in health,

even as thy soul prospereth.

If the Lord wishes we shall prosper and be healthy and that He wishes this above all things, surely when He says He is able, He is also willing. One reason for God to prosper us is so we can in turn bless others.

The other verse that spoke to me was Ephesians 3:20. Take a look.

Ephesians 3:20 (KJV)
Now unto him that is able to do
exceeding abundantly above all
that we ask or think, according to the
power that worketh in us,

This verse is amazing because it is telling us we cannot even fathom what God is able to do. However, the clause is critical in understanding the rest of the verse, because it means it is according to the power that works in us. That power comes by faith.

What does God mean here when the Bible says He is able? I honestly think God's ability to abound His grace towards us has a lot to do with the faith we place in Him. Yes, God is almighty powerful and spoke the entire world into creation. He does not need my faith for Him to do global miracles. But He requires my faith to some degree to move in my life. For example, if I am ill and I for whatever reason cannot place my faith in God that He can heal me, my healing will most likely not take place. I am not talking about those believing God for healing and are struggling to see it manifest. I am talking about those who flat out declare what the doctor said as if it is the end of it. Some people also think God picks and chooses who He wants to heal. But for whatever reason, they do not believe God will heal them. Jesus gave many examples of the importance that faith played in healing people. I surmise faith still plays a critical part today in seeing results, and it applies to how this verse works.

I talk more about healing in a later chapter. But if you are reading this and struggling with healing while trying to believe God to get well, don't give up seeking the Lord. Take an honest look at your relationship with God. How well do you know Him? It is hard for us to trust a stranger. It takes time to build a relationship to where you fully trust another person. God is no different. If you just casually know Him it is going to be hard for you to trust Him with something important like your healing. If you don't know His word, it is difficult to stand on it. Our faith in God is more stable the more we know Him and trust Him. So I encourage you to develop a deeper relationship with Him.

God being able to make all grace abound toward me is a result that happens when I place my faith in Him. Faith activates the Word of God. It means believing that if God calls me to do a good work, that He will also enable me with the means to do it.

Let's look at this again.

> And God is able to make all grace abound toward you; that ye, always having all sufficiency in all things, may abound to every good work:

One could look at this verse from a skeptic viewpoint. Wondering how they could always possess enough to always give generously to every good work when they can hardly keep up with their bills. They would conclude they would need to be a millionaire to always give that way. But that is not what this verse is saying.

What God has spoken to me on this verse is, "Tammy, when I call you to do a good work, have faith in Me that I will enable you and equip you to do that good work. If you can believe Me for that promise, then I am able to make all grace abound toward you; that you, always having all sufficiency in all things, may abound to every good work that I call you to do."

2 Corinthians 9:8 (KJV)

And God is able to make all grace abound toward you;
that ye, always having all sufficiency in all things,
may abound to every good work:

Chapter 2 : Grace

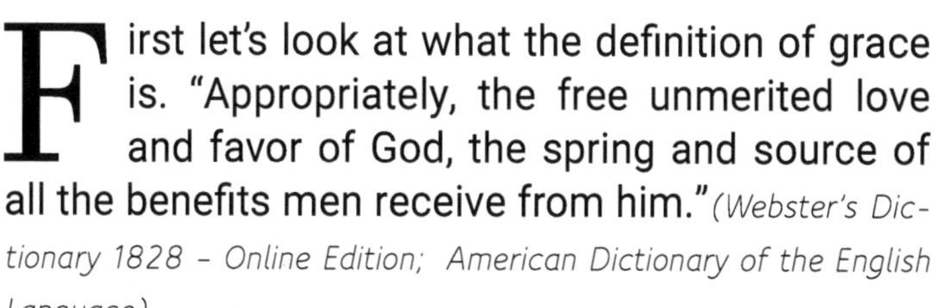

First let's look at what the definition of grace is. "Appropriately, the free unmerited love and favor of God, the spring and source of all the benefits men receive from him." *(Webster's Dictionary 1828 - Online Edition; American Dictionary of the English Language)*

Free, meaning God gives His grace without any exchange or compensation. God freely gives His love and favor to us. To us meaning, those He has given to Jesus. This is a verse for believers. How can I say that? Because Jesus said nobody comes to the Father but through Him.

John 14:6 (CSB)

Jesus told him, "I am the way, the truth, and the life. No one comes to the Father except through me."

You can't receive God's grace without going through Jesus and becoming born again. The love and grace God extended to unbelievers was His son Jesus dying for them. If you are not willing to receive that ultimate gift from God, His own son having laid down His life for you, how can you even consider coming before God to ask for more?

The grace that God is giving believers here is to equip us to be able to do good works, and we cannot do them without the strength of Christ. This is not to say you cannot do good works without God. Even unbelievers can do good works to help others like feed the poor.

But that is not what God is referring to here in good works. The grace given here is for doing those good works that God is calling you to do, and you need the strength of Christ to achieve them.

What's the difference? The main difference is God will call you to do things above your own abilities. These things God calls us to do will cause the enemy to lash out to stop you. The enemy detests us doing those good works God himself calls us to do, so brace for impact as he will oppose you when you attempt to do them.

Therefore you need the grace of God to enable you. Nonbelievers can do lots of nice and helpful things but there is a difference between doing things from a human standpoint versus doing things from God's standpoint.

In 2 Corinthians 9:8, God is saying we shall have all sufficiency in all things, so we can then abound to every good work. The sentence starts off with God is able to abound the means and ability to us. Meaning we need God's grace to help us abound to every good work. As believers we can do all things through Christ, who strengthens us.

Philippians 4:13 (KJV)

I can do all things through Christ
which strengtheneth me.

Paul wrote 2 Corinthians for believers. It is most obvious in 2 Corinthians 6:14 where it says to not be yoked together with unbelievers. If you are reading this and hungry for God's favor in your life but not sure if you are born again, this would be a good time to resolve that.

John 1:12-13 (KJV)

But as many as received him, to them gave
he power to become the sons of God,
even to them that believe on his name:
Which were born, not of blood, nor of the
will of the flesh, nor of the will
of man, but of God.

To be born again is to receive Jesus into your heart. Salvation is a gift and hence the reason we take action to receive it. This is more than an acknowledgment of who He is (the Son of God), but a desire to have your sins forgiven.

Galatians 2:20 (CSB)

I have been crucified with Christ, and I
no longer live, but Christ lives in me.
The life I now live in the body,
I live by faith in the Son of God, who
loved me and gave himself for me.

The Word says we are to repent and be born again. To repent is to have a change of heart. In the case of salvation, it is a change from unbelief to belief. The change of your heart and your faith in Jesus is what saves you.

John 3:16 (KJV)

For God so loved the world, that he
gave his only begotten Son,
that whosoever believeth in him should
not perish, but have everlasting life.

It is not so much the words you speak but what is in your heart. For God knows the hearts of men. If you want salvation and are willing to put your trust and faith in Jesus, then speak and say something like this. "Father God, I thank you for calling me to an awareness of my sin and in my heart I place my trust in your son Jesus for my salvation. Thank you for your grace in saving me. Amen."

It is that simple. Simple in that if you meant the words you spoke, you're saved. However, that is not the end but rather the beginning. We don't reach out to God, take His gift of salvation, thank Him, and return to our old lives.

God didn't *just* send His son Jesus to die for you to keep you from being separated from Him forever by going to Hell. No, the Lord longs to have a relationship with you. He already knows everything about you as He created you. What God wants is for you to know *Him*.

So how does one have a relationship with God? You spend time with God through prayer and reading His word. This is how you come to know Him. As your relationship with God grows, so will your hunger to know Him more.

It is similar to other relationships, in that you get out of it what you put into it. If you only seek a casual relationship with God, He will respect that, even though it is not His wish. His desire is to have a fulfilling relationship with you. But you set the pace for that. The more you pursue Him and read His word, the closer you will walk with God.

We have God's grace, the free unmerited love and favor of God, the spring and source of all the benefits men receive from Him, because of Jesus.

It is not based on anything we do or don't do.

Grace is unmerited, meaning I can't earn it. I can't earn more grace. I will say it a third time, I cannot earn more grace. But wow did I try! I went through a time when it seemed like I was lacking and that I needed to do something to get God's favor on my life to increase. The financial strain on my life was constant, and I felt like God was withholding favor from me. I came to God asking Him what I needed to do to earn more grace, and His favor on my life. I even at times found myself begging God to give me more grace.

Because I believed God was able, and I was not seeing the results I would have liked, I assumed it was my fault. I must be doing something wrong. This is not always the case as the enemy will try to push you back as you move towards God. During times of testing and trials the enemy will try to convince you of all kinds of negative things about yourself and your relationship with God. This is the testing. I cannot stress enough how important it is to stay in the Word and stay close to God during these times. We need a constant reminder of God's promises over us.

I came to understand that as a believer in Christ, I already have everything. This includes God's favor. From this verse 2 Corinthians 9:8, it says I have *all* His favor. The word *all* indicates everything He has. God is able to give us all He has, all His love and all His favor. Not some of it based on how good we are, but all of His free unmerited love and favor.

That's amazing, and understanding that is where the faith comes in believing He is able. God is able, and He is willing.

Once I understood this truth, it no longer made any sense that God might be withholding favor over my life. That is a lie from the enemy. It also showed me that I was in ignorance of going to God asking for more grace, when God had already given me all. I simply had to trust He was able.

On the flip side of this, at another point in my life, I experienced a level of condemnation that somehow I could screw up and stop God's love and favor on my life. Yes, the enemy will assist us in wrong thinking. The enemy does this to intervene in our trust in God and in the promises of His Word. If the enemy convinced Adam and Eve to doubt God's Word and ability in the perfect Garden of Eden, you can bet he will come against you and me even more in this fallen world we live in.

There was a time in my life where I had large amounts of house and car repairs that cost more money than I had. This went on for over a year. After many months of giving faithfully in the beginning of the month and then having to charge food on my credit card to feed my kids at the end of the month, I came to God confused. As a single mom I had come to a place where I felt I had to choose between fixing my car, fixing the water tank, feeding my kids, or giving to my local church. This bothered me.

There are scriptures saying give and you

shall receive, and then another saying you shall lend and not borrow. It baffled me that I was giving my money away and then not having it to feed my kids or repair our home.

The enemy loves to come and make us feel bad over not being good enough, and not giving enough. But God knows our hearts. Since I was little, I gave things to those in need. I remembered when I was a child giving all my Barbie dolls to this poor girl on my street who had none. When I had my first teen job in fast food, a mom working there had nothing to give her daughter for Christmas one year. I pulled out my old dollhouse full of doll furniture, and miniature dolls and gave it to her. The Holy Spirit brought back to my remembrance that I have the spirit of giving inside of me. That is what matters. Having a genuine desire to give and help others.

I know many Christians that say we should tithe no matter what. But that is legalistic and not all that God has said about giving. Above all, God wants you to have a heart for giving and to give with joy. If you are under condemnation and legalistic pressure to give no matter what, even when you don't have it or are not cheerful in giving, then it benefits you not. That is not the spirit of giving that pleases God.

1 Corinthians 13:3 (KJV)

And though I bestow all my goods to feed the poor,
and though I give my body to be burned,
and have not charity, it profiteth me nothing.

Some Christians may be thinking that I did not believe God to provide for all of it. But I had. I had been a giver of over 10% on a regular basis for many months, and after a time of the extra money not coming in to cover all my repairs and my credit card debt rising, I had to choose. This was not something I decided lightly. I did not completely stop giving, but rather reduced what I gave and I felt bad about this. This is not to say God did not provide extra. No, God supplied greatly during this time but the enemy also came against me relentlessly. The enemy enjoys making us feel condemned and unworthy. But condemnation is not from God.

However, we should not give reluctantly. That is where I had found myself. I was giving at the beginning of the month and then having to charge food on my credit card to feed my kids at the end of the month. Then at the beginning of the next month, I became more reluctant to give if it entailed me not having the means to feed my kids.

2 Corinthians 9:7 (KJV)
Every man according as he purposeth in his heart,
so let him give; not grudgingly, or of necessity:
for God loveth a cheerful giver.

Deuteronomy 16:17 (KJV)
Every man shall give as he is able,
according to the blessing of the Lord thy God which he
hath given thee.

It worried me if I did not give at least 10% at

that point, I would somehow fall out of God's grace or it would block the windows of Heaven opening to me. But God in all His love reminded me that grace is unmerited. Just like I cannot earn more grace, I can't earn less grace. The grace of God comes upon me unmerited and not based upon anything I do or don't, as again it is unmerited. I have grace because I am a believer in Christ Jesus; I am a part of His body the church. The grace that God gives me is because of what His Son did for me, not what I do or don't do.

When God looks at me, He sees me through Jesus the way He created me perfectly before the creation of the world, before I was born into sin in this fallen world. Before I became saved, sin stood between me and God, as a barrier. When I became saved, Jesus removed the sin barrier between me and God, and stands in its place. That is how God looks upon me now; through Jesus. It is important that as a believer, you understand this is how God sees you.

My intent was to use an example from my life of a time when I felt I could fall short of God's grace and not receive His blessings. I want to be clear here; I am not saying to not tithe. My heart's desire is to give abundantly and I encourage you to have a love for giving.

What I am saying is that God is not up there with a calculator in one hand and a correlating grace scale over your life in His other hand. There are many people that give from their heart on a regular basis. There are also times when opposition will strike hard and can be financially devastating. If it comes down to giving to the church or feeding your children, God would want you to take care of the lives He entrusted to you. Feeding the hungry is a good work. God was clear that caring for your family was critical.

1 Timothy 5:8 (CSB)

But if anyone does not provide for his own family, especially for his own household, he has denied the faith and is worse than an unbeliever.

There are scriptures on giving and receiving, sowing and reaping. But the verse 2 Corinthians 9:8 is so much more than the giving of money. When you give to your church, it is so the church has resources to do the good works it does. This is important. There are many Christians who faithfully write their 10% tithe check every month and that is great as churches need money to run. But that is all some Christians do. This verse is about believing in God's grace to empower you to do the good work God calls you to do.

2 Corinthians 9:8 is about *you*. God is able to make all grace abound toward *you*; that *you*, always having all sufficiency in all things, may abound to every good work. God wants to move in *your* life. He is calling you to believe in Him to empower you to do so.

2 Corinthians 9:8 (KJV)
And God is able to make all grace abound toward you;
that ye, always having all sufficiency in all things,
may abound to every good work:

Chapter 3: Abound

Let's take a closer look at what the word *abound* means as it is not commonly used in today's speech. Here is a definition of abound.

To have or possess in great quantity; to be copiously supplied; followed by with or in; as to abound with provisions; to abound in good things. To be in great plenty; to be very prevalent. *(Webster's Dictionary 1828 – Online Edition; American Dictionary of the English Language)*

God is saying He is able to give us plenty in great quantity so we can also give plenty in great quantity to every good work. He did not simply tell us to give; He told us how to give. In simple terms, He wants us to give the way He gives to us. He used the same word so there would be no confusion.

Ephesians 4:32 (KJV)
And be ye kind one to another, tenderhearted,
forgiving one another,
even as God for Christ's sake hath forgiven you.

John 15:12 (KJV)
This is my commandment, That ye love one
another, as I have loved you

God demonstrates this same principle in other examples in the Bible. He tells us to forgive others like He forgives us, and that we are to love others, as He loves us. In 2 Corinthians 9:8, He is showing that same measure. That we are to abound to others as God abounds towards us.

Toward you is also an interesting choice of words. It means to move in your favor. Not around you but towards you. And God is able to make all grace abound *toward* you, to move in your direction.

I like how the Webster's definition gives the example to abound in *good things*.

James 1:17 (CSB)
Every good and perfect gift is from above,
coming down from the Father of lights,
who does not change like shifting shadows.

When God abounds to you, it is a perfect gift from above. We are to abound good things to those good works He calls us to do.

1 Corinthians 15:58 (KJV)

Therefore, my beloved brethren, be ye stedfast,
unmoveable, always abounding in the work
of the Lord, forasmuch as ye know
that your labour is not in vain in the Lord.

Verse 1 Corinthians 15:58 instructs us to always be abounding in the work of the Lord. Not sometimes, but always abounding, and that our work for the Lord is not in vain.

Romans 15:13 (KJV)

Now the God of hope fill you with all joy
and peace in believing,
that ye may abound in hope, through
the power of the Holy Ghost.

Romans 15:13 is insightful that we may abound in hope, meaning to have a great quantity of hope. He is the God of hope. He promises to fill you with all joy, not some, but all joy and peace in believing. Why? So you can abound in hope and that it comes through the power of the Holy Ghost.

Since the power comes through the Holy Ghost, it is not something we can obtain on our own. If we could, we would not need the power of the Holy Ghost to abound in hope. The Holy Spirit in us gives us the power we do not possess without Him.

When we abound to others in good works, we are abounding hope along with it. Hope comes from God as He is the God of hope. In simple terms, when you help others you are giving them hope.

2 Corinthians 9:8 (KJV)

And God is able to make all grace abound toward you;
that ye, always having all sufficiency in all things,
may abound to every good work:

Chapter 4: Sufficiency

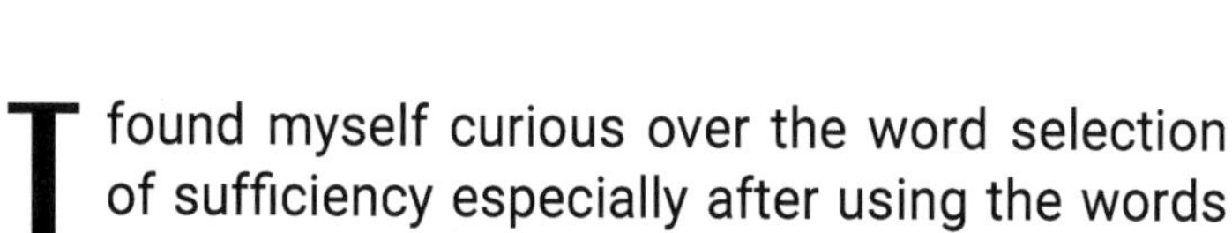

I found myself curious over the word selection of sufficiency especially after using the words *grace* and *abound* that are great and abundant. The word *sufficient* seems like it is adequate, barely enough. Here is a definition of sufficiency.

Supply equal to wants; ample stock or fund. Competence; adequate substance or means. Ability; adequate power. *(Webster's Dictionary 1828 – Online Edition; American Dictionary of the English Language)*

I wondered if He used that word for us so we don't wait until we have an abundance, but rather trust that we will have the sufficient means to abound to every good work. Again abound means to be in great plenty; to be very prevalent. So our sufficiency will be great enough to give greatly to others.

God also used *grace* and *sufficiency* together in this verse below. Our sufficiency is what God thinks is sufficient, not what we think. You will have what you need and it will be sufficient.

2 Corinthians 12:9 (CSB)

But he said to me, "My grace is sufficient for you,
for my power is perfected in weakness."
Therefore, I will most gladly boast
all the more about my weaknesses,
so that Christ's power may reside in me.

Notice that 2 Corinthians 9:8, the word *always* is inserted just before *sufficiency*. Because of His grace towards me I will always have all sufficiency in all things. He said always, not just sometimes or on special occasions. That is a huge promise and when reading this verse, one can glide over it missing this truth. But stop and look at what this means. He is saying that by His grace you will always have everything you need to abound to every good work. You won't ever lack in sufficiency.

I believe that the promises of the Bible are for those who place faith in them. If you don't believe them, they won't come true for you. Our salvation comes by our faith in Jesus that He died and rose so we too shall rise into everlasting life with Him. If you don't believe that, sadly you won't be saved. If you don't believe in healing, then sadly you won't receive healing. Here God is inviting us to believe in Him to always have all sufficiency to abound to the good works He calls us to do. He didn't say some sufficiency, He said all sufficiency. It will be adequate for what He calls us to do. Trust Him.

2 Corinthians 3:5 (KJV)

Not that we are sufficient of ourselves to
think anything as of ourselves;
but our sufficiency is of God;

2 Corinthians 9:8 (KJV)
And God is able to make all grace abound toward you;
that ye, always having all sufficiency in all things,
may abound to every good work:

Chapter 5: All Things (Money, Income, Finances, & Prosperity)

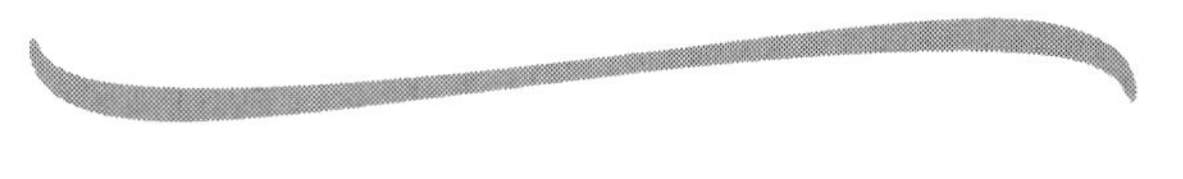

What is it to not just sometimes, but always to have all sufficiency in *all things* mean? I find this is interesting that He added *all things* in here. This opened up my mind and heart to believe for all things besides money so I could abound to every good work.

All is everything, and it became a rewarding exercise to fill in the *all things* with alternative words. These are words God gave me when I asked Him about what are some of those *all things*.

In the next several chapters I replaced the words *all things* with words that represent an aspect of that. Each chapter is a different word or words God gave me. You can see how I replaced *all things* and wrote out the verse into a declaration statement. Then I speak these over my life.

I shall always have all sufficiency in money, income, finances, and prosperity, so I may abound to every good work.

When first looking at this verse, one would deduce you would need to be wealthy to fulfill it. But upon studying the verse further, it is so much greater than only having money to give. But money is significant as it can be a tremendous blessing. Money is how we support ourselves, pay our rent, feed our family, and so forth.

John 10:10 (KJV)

The thief cometh not, but for to steal,
and to kill, and to destroy:
I am come that they might have life, and that they
might have it more abundantly.

Jesus came so we could have life, and an abundant one. Abundance is a surplus, and that allows us to share with others. Asking and believing for this is a worthy thing.

As a single mom struggling with countless financial challenges, I want to have all sufficiency in money, income, finances, and prosperity, so I may abound to every good work and provide for my family. I longed to always have all sufficiency in this area. Nobody wants lack part of the time and sufficiency at other times. No, we want all sufficiency *always* like God promised. I figured if God abounded this towards me, then I would always, not sometimes, but always possess more than enough to provide for my family and be able to abound towards others.

If I was barely getting by to take care of my family, how was I to help others financially? I felt inadequate in sufficiency to abound to every good financial work. I wanted to give, but I also wanted to provide for my family. So I spoke this over my life every morning while believing in my heart that God was able and willing to make all grace abound towards me; that I, always having all sufficiency in money, income, finances, and prosperity, may abound to every good work.

I say this because guilt tried to come against me when I asked for all sufficiency in money, income, finances, and prosperity. Yes, the enemy is very good at messing with our heads. This is why God gave us the helmet of salvation. So stick it on and rebuke the lies the enemy is telling you.

I will talk about what a good work is later in the book, but for now I will simply say that taking care of your family and the children God entrusted to you is a good work. Jesus took time to feed the thousands, and it was a good work. God wants you to be able to feed your family but also to have an abundance to abound towards others. The way I came to look at this is simple.

Asking and believing God to not just meet

your financial needs, but surpass them so you have a surplus to give others, is a good thing.

If you have your needs met, great! Then believe God for the extra to fulfill this verse. But if you don't, there is no condemnation in asking for God to meet your needs plus the extra to fulfill this verse.

When we listen to God and are obedient to him, we enable Him to move in our lives. There were certain times God would speak and tell me to give. I remember the first time this happened. I was in church and a lady was visiting from another country. She told her story of how she spent her life smuggling Bibles into a country and then ended up starting an orphanage overseas. It was a moving testimony.

I was at the time preparing to break off my engagement and move out from living in sin with my fiancé whom I knew I could not marry. So every penny counted as it would cost thousands to move.

While sitting in church listening to her, it shocked me when God said, "I want you to give her a hundred dollars."

Being stunned, I clarified with God just to make sure He did not mean ten dollars. I even reminded God how tight my money was as if He did not already know. He reconfirmed I was to give her a hundred dollars. So I pulled out my checkbook and my hand was even shaking while I wrote the check. After the service when I gave her the check, she took my hands and prayed over the offering and asked God to bless it. This was a seed I was sowing even though I did not understand that yet.

There were other times when God told me to give to visiting missionaries and the following times it was not as hard as the first time, so I did it when God told me to. Sometimes God did not ask me to give; not that their cause was not worthy, but God was not calling *me* to that good work. Perhaps on those days He was speaking to someone else.

When we step out in faith and are obedient to God, He blesses that. We are sowing a seed that will at some point return a harvest. When it came time for me to move, the day before my settlement, FHA pulled out of my loan over a blue light system on my well. The bank then told me I had to switch to a conventional loan. A conventional loan would cost me thousands more at the settlement table. It was unsettling news as I did not have the extra money.

I called my pastor asking him for prayer and direction. He said he would pray and call me back. A few moments later he called and informed me that the church had decided to give me the extra money needed so I could buy the house. Because I had stepped out in faith to stop living in sin, the church wanted to bless that. Talk about a harvest on sowing! Even though I was giving to my church regularly, that hundred dollars God asked me to sow was so I could trust Him. He wanted me to sow that seed.

A few months after I had moved, I was at the sink when God spoke to me. He said He wanted me to give a lady in my church a hundred-dollar groceries gift card, and that I was to sustain her monthly until she got Social Security. This lady became ill from her workplace and could not work anymore, but Social Security was dragging out the process and delaying in giving her benefits. At this point I did not hesitate and was joyful to help her. Had I not already learned to trust and be obedient to God in a smaller seed, I may not have been able to handle this one.

At the time of writing this chapter it has been way over a year since I heard God call me to that good work, and I continued to be obedient even through the hard times. Even through the times when I had to reduce my offering to the church and when I had to charge food for my own kids on a credit card, I continued to honor God on this. I did this because God specifically told me what to give, who to give to, and how long to give. I also believed God that my sowing would someday result in a harvest.

A harvest is also not an equal exchange. When a farmer sows a seed, God designed that seed to multiply in its harvest. Different crops return different yields, but they all return greater than the amount sown. Take, for example, a cherry tomato plant. I gardened for many years and I would grow these super sweet orange cherry tomatoes. I would save my seeds and grow them the following year. One of these tiny seeds would produce this huge tomato plant with several branching vines. On each vine, it would produce multiple clusters of cherry tomatoes, and in each tomato were handfuls of seeds. It is amazing when you comprehend the beauty of sowing that way.

I did at one time ask God why He picked me to sustain her. Not that I was being disrespectful, but I was curious. I mean here I am a struggling single mom and our church had many others in better financial situations than I was. I could not even finish my question before God so lovingly interrupted me. He said, "Tammy, I picked you to sustain her because I wanted to bless you. You know firsthand what it is like to be in need and for another person to sustain you."

Even through all my struggles, God provided money for me to abound to the good works He called me to do. It was sufficient. That is God's grace.

2 Corinthians 9:8 (KJV)
And God is able to make all grace abound toward you;
that ye, always having all sufficiency in all things,
may abound to every good work:

Chapter 6: All Things (Possessions Such as Clothing & Food)

I shall always have all sufficiency in possessions such as clothing and food, so I may abound to every good work I am called to do.

The ability to give clothing and food to those in need is a kindhearted thing to believe for the means to do so. I prayed often for my cupboards, pantry, and fridge to be full. There were many times when I wanted to bring a dish to someone who was sick or had a death in the family and yet I hardly had money to feed my kids. This troubled me. I wanted to come to a place where I could always provide food as a good work to those I am called to help.

When I started trusting God for this in my life, I was able to make a meal for a sister in Christ after surgery, provide a meal for those who had moved, and give extra eggs on Christmas morning to my neighbor who ran out when unexpected company stayed over. It is satisfying to retain provisions for readiness to give.

I remember when I was a little girl, and I went to visit a distant relative. We stayed longer than expected and as the evening came, it brought a chill. The lady we were visiting took notice of me being cold. She motioned for me to follow her upstairs in her beautiful, well-manicured home. Then she opened up her dresser drawer filled with all colors of pretty sweaters. She gestured with her hand and encouraged me to pick one. I remember how excited I was to just wear one of these beautiful soft things even for just a little while. But what struck me was when it was time to leave she smiled at me and said, "You keep it." It was such a generous, thoughtful moment in my life and yet it was just a sweater. But this is the impact a good work can have on someone. I remember how special I felt, and that is how I want to affect those I give to.

Our church has a member with an extra car, and he freely loans it out to those in need. I gratefully took him up on borrowing his car several times when mine got towed to the repair shop. It was such a huge blessing as rental cars add up in cost and going without a car even for a short time is inconvenient when you live out in the countryside. This is just another example of always having all sufficiency in possessions so you can be in a position to bless someone.

It is not selfish to want or ask for these things as it provides a way for you to provide to others. We should desire things that can help those to whom God calls us to assist.

2 Corinthians 9:8 (KJV)

And God is able to make all grace abound toward you;
that ye, always having all sufficiency in all things,
may abound to every good work:

Chapter 7: All Things (Love, Kindness, & Hospitality)

I shall always have all sufficiency in love, kindness, and hospitality, so I may abound to every good work I am called to do.

Love is a beautiful thing to believe for. I believe that I can have all sufficiency in love, so I may abound to every good work. Love is a great motivating factor to do a good work and share love with others who may not know love. But first it is important to understand where love comes from and how we are to love. Love comes from God who first loved us.

1 John 4:19 (CSB)

We love because he first loved us.

I spent a good deal of time trying to understand God's love for me. When we get a revelation of His love for us, it changes us. It changed me. I love God because He first loved me. God loved me when I did not deserve it. He loved me enough to send His only Son to die for me. After I received Christ, God spent so much time trying to get me to understand how much He loves me. He made it personal.

I remember a few years after I received salvation, and I was trying to understand how Jesus died for me. Yes, I believed He died in general for me as part of the world as stated in John 3:16. I was a part of the world; I got that part. But I struggled with how Jesus died for me personally as I was not even born yet.

I was driving to work one night as I worked the midnight shift in a rehab for teens, and this was heavy on my mind. I worked with these kids because God saved me from dying and going to Hell, but also from a teenage life of drug addiction. He reached down with His amazing love and picked me up from the lowest point in my life and gave me a new one. I was working with these teens hoping to help them start a new life.

I believe when we seek God with questions, He answers us. And so He did that night. I had this vision where I saw Jesus on the cross and His love just radiated towards me.

He looked at me and spoke these words: "I died for *you* Tammy, so that when you got on your knees in that cell, I was able to come to you." My eyes overflowed, and tears ran down my face. Jesus made it personal on a level I could understand. From that moment on I knew Jesus had died for me individually. That was a powerful revelation on the Word of God and understanding how much He loves me.

Many years later I was seeking to understand who I was in Christ and understanding God's love for me on a deeper level. I knew if I could get an unquestionable revelation of God's love for me, I could look at some of these verses I was struggling over, and not question if God would do it for me. That may seem silly to some, but I had believed for many things through a long period of hardship. When I would pray and ask, and not see the results, somewhere inside me a small voice questioned why. It was a question of God's love for me. If He loved me, then why was I going through this? Why were my prayers not being answered?

The Holy Spirit can bring back things to our remembrance like when God saved me. I remembered He loved me, but I also knew I needed a more confident knowledge of this.

First, the way I was praying was a fearful prayer. I would get overwhelmed and stressed out over huge repair bills and not know how I would get through the month and feed my kids. That is how I went to God in prayer. Crying, fearful, and begging Him to help me. Then taking verses to Him in a way of, "Your Word says this and Your promises are that. I did x, y, and z so why am I not receiving Your blessings?"

Yes, I spent months praying that way and not understanding why things were not getting better. Fear interferes with faith. Fear is not from God and it is a tool the enemy uses to place a roadblock in our prayer path.

If I believe wholeheartedly that God can handle whatever I bring to him, whether it be sickness or financial concern, then I would not feel worried or afraid when approaching God. I would come before Him with confidence knowing He can fix anything broken in my life.

Isaiah words it beautifully that we will have perfect peace because we trust in Him.

Isaiah 26:3 (KJV)

Thou wilt keep him in perfect peace,
whose mind is stayed on thee: because
he trusteth in thee.

Jesus is the Prince of Peace.

Isaiah 9:6 (KJV)

For unto us a child is born, unto us a son is given:
and the government shall be upon his shoulder:
and his name shall be called Wonderful,
Counsellor, The mighty God,
The everlasting Father, The Prince of Peace.

We can't fully grasp this peace from God as it is beyond our human understanding, but we can know that it comes through Christ.

Philippians 4:7 (KJV)

And the peace of God, which passeth
all understanding, shall keep your hearts
and minds through Christ Jesus.

Jesus said in Him is peace. Things will happen in life, but stay positive for He has overcome the world.

John 16:33 (KJV)

These things I have spoken unto you,
that in me ye might have peace.
In the world ye shall have tribulation: but be
of good cheer; I have overcome the world.

This is what He was trying to tell me about my fearful prayers. Therefore, I have come to understand that I need to find peace in Jesus that produces the confidence to go boldly before the Lord.

John 14:27 (KJV)

Peace I leave with you, my peace I give unto you:
not as the world giveth, give I unto you.
Let not your heart be troubled, neither let it be afraid.

That verse really sums this up. Do not be afraid for Jesus has given us peace. I listed an adequate sampling of verses but there are so many more on peace and trust.

God is so patient and loving in helping us to grow. He adjusts us so we can see things His way and not focus on how things look from our perspective. The process can be painful, but God allows it because He loves us and wants us to grow into a deeper relationship with Him.

It took me a long time to change how I prayed, trusting God even when I couldn't see things working out. When we trust God, we can come to Him confident and not fearful in prayer. It is impossible to please God without faith. How did I learn to trust God and overcome my fearful praying? I did so by seeking a deeper understanding of His love for me. If I comprehend how much He loved me, I could be confident and go fearlessly to the throne of God and ask my Father anything in His son Jesus' name. Not out of fear begging God, but out of faith trusting He was able and willing.

When fear tries to come against me it is my responsibility to cast it out. Jesus said in Him is peace. That is the place I want to be when I approach God. Standing with Jesus in perfect peace and submitting my request to God. I will delay praying about something until I can shake off the fear because I have learned not to come to God that way.

I could write a whole book on the process of understanding God's love and the correlating confidence it gave me in prayer. It is a process, and I am still growing in this area. But I remember one day when a moment of clarity of God's love touched me.

My youngest son and I were out running errands one afternoon and he wanted an ice cream cone from our local ice cream shop. I suggested he wait, but he said the most surprising thing.

He said with bold confidence, "Mom, at the end of the day you will buy me that cone, you just see."

So I asked him, "Why is that?"

And he replied, "Because you love me."

I pondered those words the rest of the day as we ran errands and yes, I bought him a cone because I do love him. But his words made me think. He was confident in my ability to provide for him because he knew how much I loved him. Then it hit me. At the end of the day, God will provide for me because He loves me. He always has.

I shall have all sufficiency in love means I shall not lack in love. I believe God wants me to share with others how much He loves them. It's not just unbelievers who do not know God's love for them, but even believers can go through times of testing when they may feel unloved by God because of their circumstances.

I was reading the book of John one night and these verses got my attention.

John 15:9-17 (CSB)

As the Father has loved me, I have also
loved you. Remain in my love.
If you keep my commands you will remain
in my love, just as I have kept my Father's
commands and remain in his love.
I have told you these things so that my joy
may be in you and your joy may be complete.
This is my command: Love one another as I
have loved you. No one has greater love than
this: to lay down his life for his friends.
You are my friends if you do what I command
you. I do not call you servants anymore,
because a servant doesn't know what his
master is doing. I have called you friends,
because I have made known to you everything
I have heard from my Father. You did not
choose me, but I chose you. I appointed you
to go and produce fruit
and that your fruit should remain,
so that whatever you ask the Father in my
name, he will give you. This is what I command you:
Love one another.

What got my attention about these verses is how we are to love. I saw three examples of love, and from my perspective I saw them as different levels of love. At the top was God's love for Jesus, "As the Father has loved me." When I think about how God loves Jesus, there seems to be no greater love than that. In my mind, God loves Jesus above all. But then right after that Jesus says, "I have also loved you."

Here Jesus is saying He loved us with the

same measure as God loved Him. It is easy to read over and miss this point like I did for many years. If I contemplate how God loved Jesus on one hand, and how Jesus loved me on the other, from my perspective it is hard to fathom they could be equal. I deduce God loved Jesus more. But that is not what He is saying here. Jesus is saying He loved us the same as God loved Him.

Then a few verses down Jesus says, "My command is this: Love one another as I have loved you." I have heard this before, but this time I heard it different. I heard: "Love each other the way God loved me." That seemed a much greater command. To not just love others as Jesus loved us, but to love them as God loved Jesus. Amen.

What I am getting at is to believe I can have all sufficiency in love, God's kind of love in all its powerful glory, so I may abound to every good work. Then consider how to abound that love to every good work. That is a life changer. Love can change people.

The other thing I added here is kindness. I shall always have all sufficiency in kindness, so I may abound to every good work.

Kindness is an act of love, a gentle form of it. There are many ways to be kind. Not just to those we love, but in showing kindness to strangers. Helping others, opening doors for others, picking up something they dropped, and letting people in front of you in traffic. Yes, road rage goes away when you make an effort each day to see how nice you can be in traffic.

Even the simplest form of smiling at a stranger can cause them to experience a moment of joy.

God has endless ways and opportunities each day for us to show kindness to others. There is no shortage of opportunities. Kindness can affect your mood. You can experience a horrible day and if you stop and set it aside for a moment to show kindness to others, it helps you. It is amazing how those acts of kindness can fill your own heart with joy, a joy that is big enough to swallow up the frustrations of your bad day. When you show kindness, it has an immediate benefit return.

Now let's look at hospitality, as I want to be generous on all occasions. It excites me when I can show hospitality to someone. God loves a cheerful giver. These occasions are not as frequent as kindness but since I am believing for it, I look for opportunities.

I remember booking a suite in advance at a discount price for a conference. At the last minute a friend of mine signed up for the conference but there were no vacancies. So it was a wonderful opportunity to be generous and offer hospitality inviting her to stay with me.

2 Corinthians 9:11 (CSB)

You will be enriched in every way for all generosity,
which produces thanksgiving to God through us.

There are many ways to offer hospitality to others if you are paying attention. You can bring meals to those who are sick, offer to watch the kids for a single mom who needs a break but cannot afford one, cut your elderly neighbor's grass, and so on.

The more you believe for these things, the more God will provide you with opportunities for good works in love, kindness, and hospitality.

2 Corinthians 9:8 (KJV)

And God is able to make all grace abound toward you;
that ye, always having all sufficiency in all things,
may abound to every good work:

Chapter 8: All Things (Time)

I shall always have all sufficiency in time, so I may abound to every good work I am called to do.

One day I was driving down the road analyzing this verse and asking God what are some of those *all things* and He gave me the word *time*. Wow, this one changed how I see my time in my life. I am very busy and time is precious. We all get the same twenty-four hours each day but how we use it matters.

I am always trying to figure out how to maximize my time. I spend time organizing my time with a daily calendar of list items, monthly calendar lists, and even yearly calendar lists.

We all have a friend, a co-worker, or a relative who, when their name shows up on our caller id, we speculate it will be an hour-long call at least. Then we decide within a ring or two if we have that time to spend talking to that person. I have let many calls go to voicemail because time is so valuable. When I am busy, I hoard my time. I might want to talk to that person, but not at that moment. Not everyone calls at convenient times.

But I thought about this principle. If I believe God to have all His grace, abound towards me so I can have all sufficiency in *time*, then I would have time to take the call and still finish up my work. That person calling could be struggling, needing a friend, someone to lift them up or encourage them, or help them to make a decision. So taking time for them could abound to a good work.

Getting my work done so I can reserve quality time with my children is also a good work. Good parenting is an investment in a child's future. Quality time spent with our kids is so valuable. As a single mom I long for more time to enjoy my kids, but I also need to support them, put food on the table, and work can take up much of my time. When one of my kids interrupts me while working, I need to assess the moment as to: Is this critical, can this wait, or do I want to prioritize this moment with my child?

But then there are other times when I am relaxing and wanting time for myself. Maybe the article I am reading while intriguing is not as important as time spent with my child who wants to talk with me. Instead of seeing it as an interruption, I could see it as an opportunity to trust God with my time.

Once I started believing for all sufficiency for time, I had lots of opportunities to put it into action. It's interesting how that happens. I remember texting back and forth when my youngest son sat down next to me asking to talk. There was a temptation to say, "In a minute. Let me finish this dialog texting first." But it was like God tapped me on my shoulder and reminded me of what I believed Him for. So I put my phone down and gave my son my undivided attention. It was not anything in particular we talked about; he just wanted to talk to me. It was the time I gave to my son that mattered. I was striving for more quality time with my kids and God gave me an opportunity to make that happen. How we spend our time comes down to the choices we make on a daily basis.

When I break from my busy life to give my time to someone, I am putting my faith in God surrounding time. But I am also prioritizing my time for good works.

I need to protect my valuable time, and that means learning to say no. If I do not say no to some things, I will not have the time to say yes to other things that are more important. It can be hard to let go of time hogs in our lives, especially ones we enjoy. But when we can learn to identify the main priorities in our lives, it can become easier with more practice.

This can also include letting go of good things. Yes, sometimes even good things in our lives need to go in order to do another good thing. We only get twenty-four hours each day.

I used to be a huge gardener with a greenhouse and thirty-two raised beds, and I started everything from seeds. I loved this hobby for most of my life, until it came time to give it up. God can give us the desires of our heart, but He can also change those desires. My kids and I spent hours each day watering and weeding. Then God placed this desire inside me to write the book *The Land of Good Dreams*. I was a photographer and the farm I landscaped was my outdoor studio. So you can imagine how busy I was already.

The interesting thing that happened was at the same time God gave me this new desire, He also took away my desire to garden. You might wonder why God would do that. Well if God had left both desires, I would not have been able to write as gardening took up too much time. Nobody enjoys being torn inside and frustrated. God wanted me to do something for Him, to write this book, and so He removed a huge distraction from my life to enable me to make time for it. I am grateful as it made letting go of gardening easier. It is okay to let go of what seems like a good thing, even an enjoyable thing, to make room for something more important.

Now let's talk about the importance of letting go of toxic people. My tight, close friendship circle is made up of those whom I trust to help build me up and encourage me. The world is full of people who are jealous, bitter, condescending, and judging. But my inner circle does not include those types of people. I find that I cannot afford to lose precious time dealing with people who are negative and bring me down. It is especially true for being a creative person. Nothing can kill creativity faster than the pollution seeping from a negative person. I ended a six-year engagement over this. My former fiancé could just not change, and no matter how much I tried to be the positive uplifting one in the relationship, his negativity and temper was a constant dark cloud over my life. While I was immersed in my writing, he would come home and barge into my office yelling at me. It would stop all creative flow for hours if not days. Saying he was sorry did not return my creativity.

I was writing my first book that God had placed on my heart to do. So I had to make a huge lifestyle change if I was to fulfill that purpose. And I did. God enabled me to move out from living in sin and buy my own house. When we trust God, He opens doors for us, particularly when we are willing to pick up our cross and follow him, away from sin.

Matthew 19:29 (KJV)

And every one that hath forsaken houses,
or brethren, or sisters,
or father, or mother, or wife, or children,
or lands, for my name's sake,
shall receive an hundredfold, and shall
inherit everlasting life.

So I am just going to address this here. Because I am a Christian who is writing a Christian book and just confessed to living with a man before marriage. Yes, this is because when we live in a culture that living together before marriage is acceptable, we find excuses even as Christians to justify it. The enemy will gladly jump right in and assist us in this wrong thinking. I want to put this there as I am not the only Christian who has done this, and you may be one of those people reading this book right now. Just because we get born again does not mean we learned to walk right with God immediately. It is a walk, not a sprint, and it takes effort.

For me if I go way back to when I met my ex-husband at age sixteen, I was a just-saved teen. We dated two years and lived together two years as I started my life with God. There were many things that changed overnight when I got saved such as an abrupt end to a drug addiction, but Godly understanding took much longer.

We were together twenty-three years, and those were mostly wonderful loving years until alcoholism robbed my husband of his job, his wife, his kids, his home, and then finally took his life.

My point was that when I met my ex-fiancé, a few years back, I had already had this incorrect thinking wired into my brain. After all, it worked out fine the first time; we did get married before God and had a healthy relationship for many years. But after the horrible ending I was not so eager to jump into another marriage. So I tested the waters, and we lived together.

It wasn't until I received the baptism of the Holy Spirit that a new change happened inside me. The best way to describe it was that I came alive and on fire for God. The hunger to know God and to live my life for Him grew. Along with that came a new revelation of living in sin. I remember a man at church said one day so bluntly that I busted out laughing, "If you want God to bless ya, you need to stop living in sin." But after the shock of his statement hit me, the seed of his truth spoken took root. I had this new awareness that I should not be having sex outside of marriage, and I felt it in my whole body. I also knew I couldn't marry him so the only option was to end it. God gave me grace to make that change in my life.

It may seem like I got off topic, but my point here is that sometimes making time management changes are small, like giving someone time to speak, setting our work aside, or putting the phone down. But other times it can involve a major life change.

You may work in a place that has toxic people or might be in a relationship with a negative or dishonest person. Those things can hold you back from God's best in you. You may need to believe God for a job or a relationship change. While that is a huge upset in our lives, there is a peace that comes with it in the long run.

Trusting God with my time has changed how

I see time in my life. When I believe God for all sufficiency in time, I am able to make myself available to people God may want me to bless. God is also teaching me to be a better steward of my time so I may abound to every good work He calls me to do.

2 Corinthians 9:8 (KJV)

And God is able to make all grace abound toward you;
that ye, always having all sufficiency in all things,
may abound to every good work:

Chapter 9: All Things (Energy & Strength)

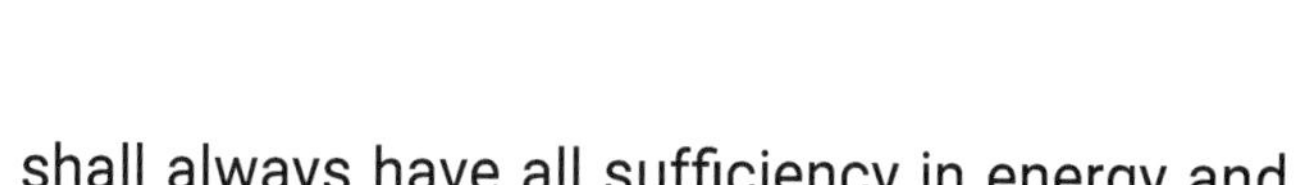

I shall always have all sufficiency in energy and strength, so I may abound to every good work I am called to do.

I can't abound to every good work if I am run down and tired. When I base my source of energy on other things besides God, I won't have all sufficiency because they are temporary crutches. I often rely on how much sleep I had, if I'm eating enough protein, caffeine consumption, or if it's sunny outside.

These things are important as we should take care of ourselves. We need proper rest and a good, healthy diet. However, many times when I feel run down and tired I go grab a cup of coffee, something sweet, or a load of protein. What if I believe God to be my source of energy and strength? If I can change my thinking from putting my trust in earthly things for energy and strength, and instead place my trust in God, then I will have all sufficiency in energy because God is able.

Every morning I speak this proclaiming it, so I can start my day off on the right foot with energy and strength. But when fatigue comes midday and my workload is high, I want to lean on God and not my caffeine. I will close my eyes and repeat this verse believing I have all sufficiency in energy. I may still grab a cup of coffee because I love it, but I want to rely on God for all my sufficiency.

As a single mom, I can easily get run down. There will be times when I will need more energy than I have so I can bless someone. This verse is saying I will always, not just sometimes, have sufficiency in energy. When this revelation hit me, I found myself more energized every day. This verse does not say you will only have sufficiency when you abound to a good work; no, it says always so that you may abound to every good work. That means you can believe for always having energy so that when a good work opportunity presents itself, you are ready.

The time in which I picked up my cross and followed Jesus was when I stopped living in sin with my ex fiancé. I had been a believer since the age of sixteen. But because of the fallen world we live in, many believers fall short and justify their sins.

God said to me one day, "If you are not going to marry him, then stop living in sin." Well I knew two years prior I could not marry him and so did God; He probably knew the whole time. But it took boldness for me to stand firm and tell my ex-fiancé I couldn't marry him, we're not having sex anymore, and I am moving out. It wasn't pleasant as my ex-fiancé did not take it well, but God gave me the ability to get through it. On my own I would not have been able to possess the courage to stand up like that.

The day before the move there was so much left to do with packing and I did not have helpers that day. So I prayed and asked God to give me the strength of a man that day. I have seven herniated disc with a metal plate holding my neck in place. I tend to have limitations. But that day God answered my prayers, and I was so strong and full of nonstop energy that I was able to get it all done.

Philippians 4:13 (KJV)
I can do all things through Christ which strengtheneth me.

All things mean more than just physical things. There are all kinds of strength such as inner strength and determination. There is mental strength when I need to super concentrate and figure out something. There is emotional strength to deal with a situation or person. Then there is long-suffering. Ouch. Yes, there is a strength that is produced from longsuffering. This is when God calls us to grow. It is unpleasant and we do not like it. But the fruit that comes from God refining us is something special. Like most people, I dislike the times of testing, but I always rejoice in what it produces in me. The changing is uncomfortable, but the results are glorious. What I learned is to believe Christ for the endurance to walk through the testing. After all, what is being produced in us is strength. God strengthens us in our walk with Him.

2 Corinthians 9:8 (KJV)
And God is able to make all grace abound toward you;
that ye, always having all sufficiency in all things,
may abound to every good work:

Chapter 10: All Things (Health, Including the Health of My Household)

I shall always have all sufficiency in health, including the health of my household so I may abound to every good work I am called to do.

You can't be much help to others when bogged down with a sickness or caring for a sick member of your household. There are verses to stand on when proclaiming health over your household.

Psalm 91:10 (KJV)
There shall no evil befall thee, neither shall
any plague come nigh thy dwelling.

When I started speaking this out loud, proclaiming it over myself and my household, I noticed an improvement in our health. What I was doing was speaking health and wellness over my family. Being healthy enables me physically to abound to every good work.

You may be wondering while reading this, what is she talking about speaking it out loud?

Proverbs 18:21 (KJV)

Death and life are in the power of the tongue:
and they that love it shall eat the fruit thereof.

I speak these things over my life because the Word says I have life and death in the tongue.

Matthew 21:21 (KJV)

Jesus answered and said unto them, Verily
I say unto you, If ye have faith,
and doubt not, ye shall not only do this which
is done to the fig tree, but also if ye shall
say unto this mountain, Be thou removed, and
be thou cast into the sea; it shall be done.

Mark 11:23 (KJV)

For verily I say unto you, That whosoever
shall say unto this mountain,
Be thou removed, and be thou cast into the sea;
and shall not doubt in his heart,
but shall believe that those things which he
saith shall come to pass;
he shall have whatsoever he saith.

The Bible records this moment twice in case we missed it the first time. These verses are talking about believing in our words that we speak from our hearts, and we shall have what we say. God spoke the world into creation. Our words have power, which is why I put into practice speaking certain things over my life.

Psalm 91:14-16 (CSB)

Because he has his heart set on me,
I will deliver him; I will protect him because he knows my name. When he calls out to me, I will answer him; I will be with him in trouble.
I will rescue him and give him honor.
I will satisfy him with a long life
and show him my salvation.

Psalm 91 is one of my favorite Psalms and I love the ending. I claim this promise from God and I speak it over my life. At the time of writing this I will turn fifty this year. It means I am about to begin the second half of my life as I expect in my heart to live to be at least one hundred. Why? Because I stand on this verse. I speak it out loud, replacing the word *he* with *she*, and *him* with *her*. Then I listen to those words come out of my mouth as if God is speaking them over me with sweet tender love.

Because I believe for this, when I hear of illnesses or things that happen to older folks, I declare them not for me. When I get a pain and a thought tries to ignite fear in me that it could be this or that disease, I rebuke it. I speak to my pain and I tell it that it is nothing but a symptom of a lie and I refuse to let fear take root in my thoughts. Then I go right back to this sweet promise from God. I believe God for longevity.

Some folks might regard this as unrealistic to believe for. But in the Bible, men of God believed for much more. Noah believed God that a flood would come upon the earth without ever seeing rain. Abraham believed God for a son when his wife was barren and past the childbearing age. Moses believed God that if he went before Pharaoh he would set the slaves free. So believing for long life when you consider it is rather small in comparison. If God kept His word to them, I can trust God to keep the promises to me.

2 Corinthians 9:8 (KJV)

And God is able to make all grace abound toward you;
that ye, always having all sufficiency in all things,
may abound to every good work:

Chapter 11: All Things (Faith, Healing, & Miracles)

I shall always have all sufficiency in faith, healing, and miracles, so I may abound to every good work I am called to do.

This may be surprising for those of you who don't believe in healing and miracles in this present day. Or you may believe that God could heal but not sure how He heals.

But let's start with faith. It is impossible to please God without faith.

Hebrews 11:6 (KJV)

But without faith it is impossible to please
him: for he that cometh to God must believe

that he is, and that he is a rewarder of them that diligently seek him.

My faith can move mountains. My faith activates the Word of God.

We live in a fallen world and we will encounter hardships that come against us. The Bible says *when*, not *if*. The closer you walk towards God, the heavier the attacks against you will come from the enemy. During our longsuffering is when we build up our faith. Jesus said we just need faith the size of a mustard seed, yet He taught a great deal on unbelief. They are two different things, and unbelief can counter your faith. I can believe God for something, and yet my circumstance around me can speak unbelief, and doubt. Things like a doctor's report, the pain your body feels, physical symptoms, and fear. This is what Jesus was teaching. He was telling us it is not your faith that is hindering you, as you just need little faith. But it is all your unbelief that is overshadowing your faith.

When I speak this over my life each day, I believe God to give me enough faith today to abound to every good work. To have faith in my abilities, faith in my health, and faith to believe God no matter what comes up against me. His sufficiency is enough.

It is important for me to remember that I only need enough faith to get me through today. That today I cast my worries on God and today I rest in His ability. My faith is in God. I say this because I find that when I worry about tomorrow, next week, next month, or next year, my faith is more tempted to falter.

In the Lord's Prayer Jesus tells us how to pray. Notice He says, "Give us today our daily bread." He did not say weekly bread, monthly bread, or retirement bread. It is because we are to place our trust in Him daily.

Matthew 6:9-13 (KJV)

After this manner therefore pray ye:
Our Father which art in heaven, Hallowed be
thy name. Thy kingdom come, Thy will be done
in earth, as it is in heaven.
Give us this day our daily bread.
And forgive us our debts, as we forgive
our debtors. And lead us not into temptation, but
deliver us from evil: For thine is the kingdom,
and the power, and the glory, for ever. Amen.

I joke that I am in the manna phase of life, where each day God gives me just enough. But in all seriousness, it is a good way to live, trusting God for that one day before you. He even goes into great detail in Matthew on not worrying about what to eat or wear and stressing that today has enough trouble of its own to not even focus on tomorrow.

Matthew 6:25-34 (CSB)

Therefore I tell you: Don't worry about your life, what

you will eat or what you will drink;
or about your body, what you will wear. Isn't life more
than food and the body more than clothing?
Consider the birds of the sky: They don't sow
or reap or gather into barns,
yet your heavenly Father feeds them.
Aren't you worth more than they?
Can any of you add one moment to his life
span by worrying? And why do you worry
about clothes? Observe how the wildflowers
of the field grow: They don't labor or spin thread.
Yet I tell you that not even Solomon in all his
splendor was adorned like one of these. If that's
how God clothes the grass of the field,
which is here today and thrown into the furnace
tomorrow, won't he do much more for you—you
of little faith? So don't worry, saying, 'What will
we eat?' or 'What will we drink?' or 'What will we
wear?' For the Gentiles eagerly seek all these
things, and your heavenly Father knows that
you need them. But seek first the kingdom of God
and his righteousness, and all these things
will be provided for you. Therefore don't worry
about tomorrow, because tomorrow
will worry about itself. Each day has enough
trouble of its own.

Now let's talk about faith in healing. This is a struggle for many people and even myself at one point. There was a time when I was so afraid that something would happen to me, causing me to die, and I worried who would raise my kids. This fear overtook my life until I learned how to rebuke it.

The enemy loves it when we fear, because it

shows a lack of faith and gives him an invitation to take advantage of us. Fear is not from God.

2 Timothy 1:7 (KJV)
For God hath not given us the spirit of fear; but of power, and of love, and of a sound mind.

Notice how He calls it the spirit of fear. The spirit of fear comes from the enemy. But God gives us power and thus we are to use that power to cast out fear.

But prior to learning this, due to ignorance, I let fear control my life. Within a year I had become like a hypochondriac, and it is an expensive fear to take hold of you. It started with when I felt a lump in my breast. The fear took me hostage, and I conceived the worst, causing panic to set in. I remember praying but my prayers were not prayers of faith, but prayers of fear. I was so worried, but I kept my focus on God, believing in healing. As time passed in those two weeks waiting to go see the doctor, I noticed my lump getting smaller and smaller until when I went to the doctor and she could not find it. It was encouraging to feel the lump go away as it strengthened my faith.

When I left the doctor, I had a sense of relief but deep down inside, without me knowing it, fear had taken root. Things began to happen to me left and right. I got essential oil in my eye and was terrified I would go blind. The enemy took note on that and messed with my vision for months, escalating that fear. My doctor found skin cancer on my forehead and I had it surgically removed. I was falling apart at the seams. Any pain and I jumped straight to "It's terminal!"

Then God sent me a message. My mother sent me a video to watch from Andrew Wommack called *God Wants You Well*. I didn't open it when I got it. But one day, I had this urgency to find the video and view it. It set me on course to a whole new way of living and trusting God. This is when I started trusting God over my fear.

I remember early on when I was trying so hard to let go of the fear and believe that God wanted me well above all things. I was lying in bed having a panic attack about my health and praying, trying to overcome it. Suddenly I heard Jesus speak loud and assertive, "Get your hands off her, she belongs to me!" It stopped the attack and I remember being puzzled as I had only ever heard Jesus' comforting voice, not His voice of authority. God says He can rebuke the devourer for our sakes.

There was another time I was studying the healing from His stripes, meaning when Jesus took our sickness upon Him one lash at a time.

Isaiah 53:5 (KJV)

But he was wounded for our transgressions,
he was bruised for our iniquities:
the chastisement of our peace was upon him;
and with his stripes we are healed.

Isaiah prophesied seven hundred years before Jesus, about Christ wounded for our transgressions and bruised for our iniquities, meaning our sins. And he added that with His stripes we are healed. He did not say *would* be healed, he said *are* healed. Why would Isaiah use present tense when making this prophesy? Perhaps he had so much faith in God and in God's Word and promise, that when God said so, Isaiah understood it was so. That even though this had not happened yet on earth, for Isaiah and his faith it was done.

Then in 1 Peter he also states how Jesus took our sins on the cross. He says by the stripes Jesus took, we *were* healed, because it happened two thousand years ago. That is when Jesus did it.

1 Peter 2:24 (KJV)

Who his own self bare our sins in his own
body on the tree, that we,
being dead to sins, should live unto
righteousness: by whose stripes ye were healed.

I love how God always tries to make it personal with me when I seek Him on understanding His word. Deep in my heart I wanted to believe that verse that Jesus had already paid for my healing with the stripes on His back. I was sitting up in bed with my Bible on my knees when this vision overtook me. Right before me I saw Jesus on His knees bound and beaten. Then I witnessed the whip come down on His back and His flesh torn open. He raised

His head up and looked right at me and said with so much love, "I took this one for you." The vision vanished as I sucked in a gasp of air and then burst into tears sobbing at what God had just showed me. Jesus reached out to me personally that day with a message, "Yes Tammy, I took a strip for you. Believe in me." He suffered for me to provide healing if I will trust Him with it.

So yes, I shall have all sufficiency in healing. Not just healing in me but to lay hands on others to heal.

Psalm 103:3 (CSB)

He forgives all your iniquity;
he heals all your diseases.

God said He heals *all diseases* and Jesus never refused to heal anyone when He walked the earth. Praise God.

Now let's discuss faith in miracles. I choose to believe in them so I can abound to that good work. He commanded us to love one another as He loves us. Jesus also told us to heal the sick, raise the dead, and cast out devils. They are more than promises of what we could do; they are commands. Why would I disregard these commands?

Matthew 10:8 (KJV)

Heal the sick, cleanse the lepers, raise the dead, cast out devils:
freely ye have received, freely give.

Jesus said that those who believe in Him will not only do what Jesus did, but greater works. What did Jesus do? He healed the sick, raised the dead, miraculously fed thousands of people, walked on water, and calmed a storm. Jesus performed lots of miracles and we who place our faith in Him are able to do these things as well plus more.

John 14:12 (KJV)

Verily, verily, I say unto you, He that believeth
on me, the works that I do shall
he do also; and greater works than these
shall he do; because I go unto my Father.

I do not presume that Jesus placed a time stamp or expiration date on performing miracles. Look at these two verses.

Mark 16:15-18 (KJV)

And he said unto them, Go ye into all the world,
and preach the gospel to every creature.
He that believeth and is baptized shall be saved;
but he that believeth not shall be damned.
And these signs shall follow them that believe;
In my name shall they cast out devils; they shall
speak with new tongues; They shall take up
serpents; and if they drink any deadly thing,
it shall not hurt them; they shall lay hands on
the sick, and they shall recover.

Matthew 24:14 (KJV)

And this gospel of the kingdom shall be preached
in all the world for a witness unto all nations;

and then shall the end come.

He told us to go into all the word to preach the gospel to everyone. Then He said the signs that will follow those that believe will be that in His name they cast out devils, speak in new tongues, lay hands on the sick and they shall recover. In the other verse He says that the end will not come until mankind preaches the gospel in all the world. So the command He gave to preach the gospel to the entire world is not complete yet, or the end would have come. So the signs that follow those who believe are still part of that promise.

I surmise the reason we are not seeing as many miracles in present time is not because they cannot happen, but people lack the faith for them to come to pass.

Ephesians 3:20 (KJV)

Now unto him that is able to do exceeding
abundantly above all that we ask or think, according
to the power that worketh in us,

Faith is the fuel to the power inside of us. Jesus gave us power and authority to use in *His name*. We are not doing these miracles on our own, but with the power Jesus gave us in His name.

Luke 10:19 (KJV)

Behold, I give unto you power to tread
on serpents and scorpions,
and over all the power of the enemy:
and nothing shall by any means hurt you.

Acts 4:30 (CSB)
while you stretch out your hand for healing,
and signs and wonders
are performed through the name
of your holy servant Jesus.

I want to have all sufficiency in faith, healing, and miracles, so I may abound to every good work. I want to be able to heal the sick, raise the dead, or any other miraculous work God calls me to do.

2 Corinthians 9:8 (KJV)

And God is able to make all grace abound toward you;
that ye, always having all sufficiency in all things,
may abound to every good work:

Chapter 12: All Things (Encouragement & Confidence in the Lord)

I shall always have all sufficiency in encouragement and confidence in the Lord, so I may abound to every good work I am called to do.

I felt inadequate at times, wondering how I am to build up others in the Lord when I was feeling discouraged. I knew God had called me to encourage others. I knew I needed to build my faith in encouragement and confidence in the Lord. Some Christians might be stunned at that statement and wonder how I can be a Christian and at the same time question my confidence in God.

Times of testing can bring us to a point when things happen that we do not understand. When we try to live right and yet bad things happen to us, a part of us wants go to God asking "Why?" That is a confidence issue. Because if we had perfect confidence in the Lord, we would never question anything; we would endure while trusting fully in Him. We do not start with that kind of built-up faith. That only comes from longsuffering, when we learn to trust God in the storm, through an illness, a failed relationship, or through financial struggle.

I was asking God how I could ever encourage anyone when I was struggling with it myself. That is why I added these words of encouragement and confidence to my list to have all sufficiency in.

I spoke this out loud every morning for many months before it took root in my heart. I had uncertainty when I went through a yearlong testing of financial strain. If something could break, the enemy broke it. My fridge leaked, part of my roof blew off, the dishwasher overflowed, the water tank died, my car was in and out of the shop with thousands in repair bills, and I had multiple computer repairs. Those were just the highlights on the extensive list, and this was before I had to rip out and replace the kitchen. I remember going over the list with God one day and He stopped me in the middle of it and said, "And I provided for that, Tammy." His words caused me to pause a minute and consider but I continued down the list. God kept responding to the list items that had come against me. "I provided the person to fix the roof; I provided the means to replace that." So I stopped and looked again at my list. God was there for all of it, and looking back I have no idea how I paid for it all, but God reminded me of His provision.

I remember hearing this preacher one day say, "It is not up to me to tell God how to bless me; it is just my job to believe that He can." Those words impacted me. I had been giving God suggestions on how He could help me. If I sold this or if things stopped breaking, or I just had another client, or my books would sell more copies. Seriously, this made me take a step back and reflect. I was fearfully praying to God. When I surrendered and said, "God, I have no clue how you are going to raise me above my circumstances, but I believe that you can," I had peace and my faith took a new course. I do not need to worry over how it will happen. That is a huge distraction, and the enemy loves to distract us. God told me once in church during praise and worship to stay on course and do not waver. God is an amazing GPS. He will course-correct me when I get lost or off the road I should be on.

I wanted to get to where I can help others to find encouragement and confidence in the Lord. I knew I needed to strengthen my confidence in God that when things came against me, I didn't run into my office and cry out in frustration demanding, "Why, God?" But rather be at a point where I was less shakable.

Around this time, God spoke to me and I found it humbling. He said, "Tammy, if you want to become unshakable, you're going to have to be shaken a few times until you learn to withstand the blows." This was profound, as if God was allowing this training process in my life so He could strengthen me.

I wanted to be at a place that when things happen, I take a deep breath, pray, and then move on, trusting God. Am I there yet? No, not completely, but I am making progress.

It is no surprise we don't learn how to do that without having to walk through it ourselves first. We don't master this through little bumps in the road, but rather through longsuffering. I know we kick and scream, not wanting to go through these times of testing. But through this, God molds us in His hands. It is like God's boot camp for us. If you're going to walk close to God, you need to get through basic training before you can enter into the Special Forces. These trials help us to endure what's coming later and to allow us to share and encourage others.

Isaiah 41:10 (CSB)

Do not fear, for I am with you;
do not be afraid, for I am your God.
I will strengthen you; I will help you;
I will hold on to you with my righteous right hand.

This verse became an anchor in the storm for me. I am not alone in any trial in my life. I can speak this verse in confidence that God is with me. He strengthens me, helps me, and I do not fear as He holds me in His righteous right hand. His right hand is special, for at His right hand sits Jesus.

Galatians 6:9 (CSB)

Let us not get tired of doing good, for we will reap at the proper time if we don't give up.

In Galatians 6:9 there is a promise in the word *will*. God has promised a harvest but at the proper time. Then notice the condition of that promise, the word *if*. If what? If we do not give up. When we have sowed a seed, watered it, weeded it, fertilized it, and are waiting for the harvest to come in, we must not become weary. Remember, God's promise is to those who stay the course and who do not give up! Those are the ones who will receive the harvest. It is a time of testing of our faith in God.

I read this verse for months before I noticed the words *the proper time*. I wanted the harvest, and I did all I could to make it happen. When the harvest did not come, I got frustrated with God and felt like He had withheld blessings from me. I kept reading that verse, focused on the *will reap* part, and wondered why I hadn't. So I shifted my focus to the words *don't give up*, but all that did was push me harder to make the harvest come sooner.

When the words *the proper time* got my attention, I finally surrendered knowing that God would bring a harvest if I did not give up, but it would be at the proper time He has set. A time when God perceives I am ready to receive it. So I can rest in Him and let go of trying to control making my harvest happen.

Remembering past trials where God saw me through helps reminds me to not give up. If He got me through that time, surely I can come through this. Another part is being in the Word and studying how God moved in others. If God did it for them, He can do it for me.

My confidence grew through the financial hardship. Believing that God is able and willing strengthens my encouragement and confidence in Him and my ability to endure.

2 Corinthians 9:8 (KJV)

And God is able to make all grace abound toward you; that ye, always having all sufficiency in all things, may abound to every good work:

Chapter 13 : All Things (Courage)

I shall always have all sufficiency in courage, so I may abound to every good work I am called to do.

Many people perceive courage as going into battle. We are indeed in a battle but it is not a physical battle, but one against the evilness in this world.

Ephesians 6:10-18 (KJV)

Finally, my brethren, be strong in the Lord, and in the power of his might. Put on the whole armour of God, that ye may be able to stand against the wiles of the devil. For we wrestle not against flesh and blood, but against principalities, against powers, against the rulers of the darkness of this world, against spiritual wickedness in high places. Wherefore take unto you the whole armour of God, that ye may be able to withstand in the evil day,

and having done all, to stand. Stand therefore,
having your loins girt about with truth,
and having on the breastplate of righteousness;
And your feet shod with the preparation of the
gospel of peace; Above all, taking the shield of faith,
wherewith ye shall be able to quench all the fiery
darts of the wicked. And take the helmet of
salvation, and the sword of the Spirit, which is the word
of God: Praying always with all prayer and supplication
in the Spirit, and watching thereunto with all
perseverance and supplication for all saints;

God prepares us for the battle. He did not say *if* it comes; He said *when* the day of evil comes. God loves us so much that He clothes us in His armor. Now contemplate that for a moment. What is God's armor that He clothes us with to be ready for battle? It is truth, righteousness, peace, faith, salvation, and the Word of God. Those are powerful things to provide us with to protect and help us battle the enemy. That is all we need to overcome the enemy, but we need all of it. He said to put on the whole armor of God.

But courage can be more subtle than that. It takes courage to speak out the truth. Jesus said He was the truth.

John 14:6 (KJV)

Jesus saith unto him, I am the way, the truth,
and the life: no man cometh unto the
Father, but by me.

We are to take the truth and speak it. Speak it with courage. The light shines the truth. I believe when we speak the truth it becomes a light that goes out into the world.

Matthew 5:15-16 (KJV)

Neither do men light a candle, and put it
under a bushel, but on a candlestick;
and it giveth light unto all that are in the
house. Let your light so shine before men, that
they may see your good works,
and glorify your Father which is in heaven.

This is the last *all things* word God gave while writing this book. Most of the words God gave me before I even started this book. I think it is interesting He waited to present this word till I began the process of this book. It took courage to write this book and send it out there in the world. We live in a time of opposition against Christians, where many people hate to hear the truth and wish to silence those who speak about God and God's truth. I believe God gave me the word courage to encourage me. Have you ever noticed the word *encourage* has *courage* in it?

I will believe for all sufficiency in courage so that when I need to speak the truth, I will not care who I offend. Because there might be that one person in the room who needs to hear the truth, and if I don't speak it, they may never hear it. So be bold and be courageous in the Lord.

Chapters 14-19 were ones for my businesses.

At the time of writing this book, I still have my photography business and a new writing career. I felt I needed certain *all things* for my business-related areas so I could be better at them, and hence why I separated them into the following chapters.

If you have a business, then these may be helpful to you or even if you do not, they can help you in your career to be successful. After all, the work that we do is what brings in our income. We all want to be prosperous so we can have a roof over our heads, feed our family, and have an abundance to give to others.

2 Corinthians 9:8 (KJV)

And God is able to make all grace abound toward you;
that ye, always having all sufficiency in all things,
may abound to every good work:

Chapter 14: All Things (Wisdom & Knowledge)

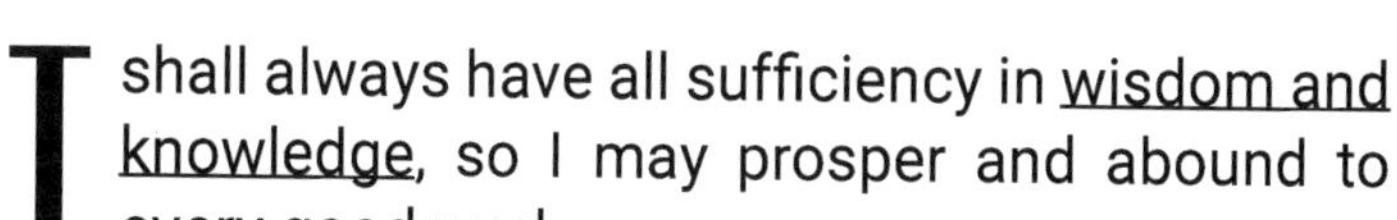

I shall always have all sufficiency in wisdom and knowledge, so I may prosper and abound to every good work.

I come to God and I speak this over my life, believing that God will provide me with all wisdom and knowledge to do my work, so my work can prosper and allow me to abound to every good work.

To run any business or to prosper at your job, you need to have all sufficiency in wisdom and knowledge. These are things we can ask God for. As a Christian running a business, I want to make sure I have wisdom and knowledge to not only do the detailed work but also to make good business decisions.

James 1:5 (KJV)

If any of you lack wisdom, let him ask of God, that giveth to all men liberally, and upbraideth not; and it shall be given him.

Right there it says we are to ask God for wisdom and He will give it to us. In such a competitive world, being prepared and equipped in your area of work is essential. The more you grow in wisdom and knowledge in your profession, the better work you will produce. There is a confidence that comes with experience, a confidence that overshadows the doubt in your abilities. But when you are new to an area of work or just learning, it can be stressful. So ask the Lord to fill you with the wisdom and knowledge you need to succeed.

Proverbs 2:6 (KJV)

For the Lord giveth wisdom: out of his mouth cometh knowledge and understanding.

1 Corinthians 2:16 (KJV)

For who hath known the mind of the Lord, that he may instruct him? but we have the mind of Christ.

We have the mind of Christ. Have you ever thought about that? How He knows all things? Many times I have asked God to help me not screw up something I am working on, or to help me grasp what I am struggling to comprehend. I remember the difficulty I had when trying to learn video to enhance my photography company. As a photographer I understood how to capture a moment and freeze it in time. Videography is capturing moments in motion. I had certain areas of difficulty such as maintaining focus on a moving person. There was frustration over not getting or understanding what I was missing and I wanted it to come quickly with instant knowledge.

I cried out many times to the Lord to help me grasp it, to help me understand what I was missing. One day the clarity came and with a sound mind in concepts that I used to find confusing.

Sometimes we rely too much on our own understanding and then get confused when we struggle. God knows all things, and He is willing and able to assist us when we ask for wisdom and knowledge.

2 Corinthians 9:8 (KJV)

And God is able to make all grace abound toward you;
that ye, always having all sufficiency in all things,
may abound to every good work:

Chapter 15: All Things (Talent & Skills)

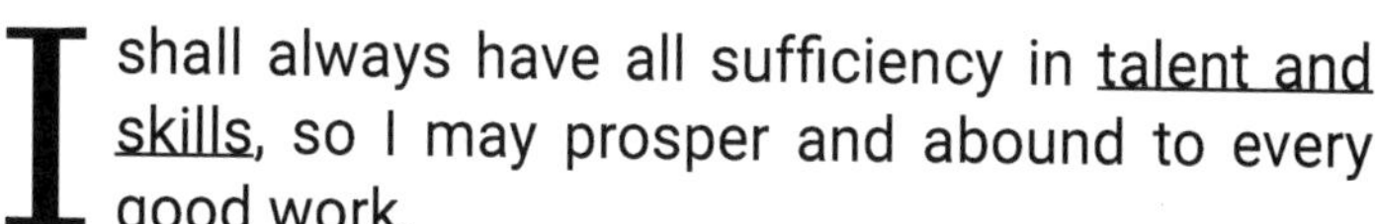

I shall always have all sufficiency in talent and skills, so I may prosper and abound to every good work.

I come to God and I speak this over my life, believing that God will bless me with the right talent and equip me with the necessary skills to do my job, so I can prosper and abound to every good work.

Ever since I can remember I have drawn. I believe that all my artistic ability comes from God. Some years back, I became an award-winning photographer, and I give all the credit to God for the gift of vision. Being able to see through the lens and capture a creative image is a gift. There is some skill involved but without the gift of vision, the image, while correct according to photographic standards, would be boring and lacking impact. I am also an excellent editor of images and I thank God for that ability. Having that skill of editing has helped my photography business as well.

I love to make things look beautiful and I have a desire to create things. God made us in His image and God is a creator of beautiful things. I realized it was a gift many years ago before my kids were born. I used to think everyone had a sense of how to make things look pretty.

I was organizing a baby shower for my sister-in-law and I gave her some decorations to go decorate the windows. She hung the garland, but it was not pretty; it was just hung. I remember looking at it confused and trying to form the right words. So I suggested that it might look better if she were to twist it into a swag. I was hoping to not hurt her feelings on the job she did. She looked puzzled and said that I should do it because she did not know how to make it look good. How could she not know what looks good? How could anyone not know? It was such a huge part of my inner being.

With the realization that it was a gift also came the understanding that if God ever took it away, I would feel completely lost. That is how much artistic creativity is a part of me.

I am also a very organized person. So when disorganization, clutter, and unplanned events come up in my life, I struggle. Having things unorganized can even hinder my other gift of creativity. I can plan an event to the very tiny details. However, with last-minute plans I am dumbfounded. I figured this out on one of my wedding anniversaries when we wanted to dine at a restaurant out in the country. We always celebrated our anniversary on the date. This time it was on a Monday. I figured being on a Monday we did not need to call and make reservations. This was back before cell phones and internet. We dressed up and drove all the way out into the country to find a dark, deserted restaurant closed on Mondays. My husband asked me where I wanted to go and for the life of me I could not think. But spontaneity was one of his gifts and so I told him to just pick. His way of picking was just driving into the closest city and finding a place that looked good. And we found an amazing restaurant that night.

I have also discovered that I am a good storyteller. God had been planting stories inside me for decades, but I didn't know what they were exactly. At times I would zone out and fantasize, watching scenes play out in my head. These stories were so vivid and filled with intense emotions that they became a part of me, tucked away. As a result, I started pursuing the dream inside me to become a full-time writer.

Those are some of my talents and skills God has given me. I am sure God gives each one of us gifts and talents, but they are not the same. God gives these gifts with a purpose and to equip you to do the good works He has in store for you.

The first part is discovering what talents and

skills God gave you. Then to believe God is able to make all grace abound toward you; that ye, always having all sufficiency in these talents and skills, may abound to every good work. One way to abound to good works is to become prosperous using your talents and skills to produce an abundant living.

But even greater is to believe for these talents and skills in themselves to abound to every good work. What I mean is I want to use my talent and skills to directly produce good works. I desire not just to be prosperous from the books I create to give me the means to abound to every good work. I also want my books in themselves to be a blessing to those who read them.

I want all sufficiency in creative writing and artistic ability, and even in my organizational skills, to result in producing good works.

God gave us these gifts, skills, and talents for the purposes He created us to do. He created us to do good works. So I speak these things over my life each morning, before I start working.

2 Corinthians 9:8 (KJV)
And God is able to make all grace abound toward you;
that ye, always having all sufficiency in all things,
may abound to every good work:

Chapter 16: All Things (Motivation & Endurance)

I shall always have all sufficiency in motivation and endurance, so I may prosper and abound to every good work.

I come to God and I speak this over my life, believing that God will help me maintain motivation and assist me in enduring in my labor, so my work can prosper and allow me to abound to every good work.

These two I paired together as they seemed fitting. Motivation in the beginning is much easier than maintaining it during hard times, such as when you're working long hours and it looks as if you're not getting anywhere, or when your business is not growing and you are wondering if you are wasting your time and money.

Genesis 8:22 (KJV)

While the earth remaineth, seedtime and
harvest, and cold and heat,
and summer and winter, and day and
night shall not cease.

There is a seedtime and harvest but waiting for the harvest is seldom easy. These are the times when you need to believe for motivation to keep you from giving up. This is also the time to ask God to help you with enduring the testing.

When I was nearing the completion of my book *The Land of Good Dreams*, I was feeling worn out. I remember a day with deep blue skies and fluffy white clouds. I had just gotten home from being gone most of the day and I felt tired. But the sky had not been this perfect for my book cover in weeks and I was running out of time to capture it. The last thing I felt up to doing was going back out to photograph the sky, and yet I knew I needed to. I might not have another opportunity for weeks and so I did what I needed to do.

As I was walking and photographing, I was complaining to God about how much hard work was going into this book. God just gave me one word, *diligence*. It stopped me in my tracks. I had heard of the word but I did not understand it. It is not a word I use in conversation.

I took note and then continued my walk, taking pictures of the sky while trying to stay awake. I had been working many late nights for weeks, and sleep deprivation was prying into my life. When I am tired, I tend to complain. I dislike being tired unless I am trying to go to sleep at night. Otherwise I find it annoying. So here I am grumbling once more to God, asking why this book had become so much work. Again God gave me the same word, *diligence*.

When I got home from photographing the sky, I looked up that word *diligence*. It means careful and persistent work or effort.

The message God gave me that day was that He wanted me to have a careful and persistent work or effort towards my book. It taught me how God wants me to work on things, and I can apply that same diligence to all things I do in my profession.

Having a successful business or a thriving career is hard work. Often years go by before we see a return on that investment.

1 Thessalonians 1:3 (CSB)
We recall, in the presence of our God and
Father, your work produced by faith,
your labor motivated by love, and your
endurance inspired by hope
in our Lord Jesus Christ.

Whatever your work is, motivate it out of

love. Let your endurance be because you keep your focus on the Lord. Don't let yourself become discouraged but keep a positive attitude by letting your labor be for God and not for men.

Ephesians 6:7 (CSB)

Serve with a good attitude, as to the Lord and not to people,

2 Corinthians 9:8 (KJV)

And God is able to make all grace abound toward you;
that ye, always having all sufficiency in all things,
may abound to every good work:

Chapter 17: All Things (Concentration, Focus, & Alertness)

I shall always have all sufficiency in concentration, focus, and alertness, so I may prosper and abound to every good work.

I come to God and I speak this over my life, believing that God will help me be able to concentrate on my work, to be able to focus on my work, and to be alert while working, so I can prosper and abound to every good work.

Our world today is full of many distractions. It is full of constant noise from social media and smartphones. Technology is supposed to help us be more efficient, yet it seems to grab our attention away from important tasks.

But life can throw us other distractions too, like a troubled marriage, a sick loved one, or financial struggles. So we need God's help in being able to concentrate, focus, and stay alert to do the work we need to do.

Sometimes it's hard to focus on your goals and concentrate at work. You may even feel exhausted and lack alertness. Taking care of yourself with a proper diet and enough sleep is an obvious remedy, but we can also rely on our Lord to help us. We may not always be able to get the right amount of sleep and eat the best way. Life can have many unexpected things come against us. We may not always be able to step away from our work even during tough, troublesome times. At these times we need to rest in Jesus, and ask Him to help us concentrate on the task at hand, to keep our minds focused on our goals, and to stay alert despite fatigue. God will never leave us nor forsake us.

Deuteronomy 31:6 (CSB)

Be strong and courageous; don't be terrified or afraid of them. For the Lord your God is the one who will go with you; he will not leave you or abandon you.

I remember a time when my youngest son had been sick with a stomach problem over several weeks and was in and out of the hospital. I would stay with him in the hospital sleeping on a couch beside his bed. But sleep was difficult. I remember one night in particular when we arrived back home and he was finally asleep. I needed to rest so badly but I had been in this constant state of urgency for so long I couldn't rest. Then as if Jesus was standing right beside my bed talking to me, I knew I needed to surrender it all to Him. But because my son was not well yet, I wasn't ready to let go. I felt restless knowing his sickness was not over yet. Jesus understood this and He did not condemn me for not surrendering all my worry and stress to Him. Instead He said the sweetest, most loving thing. He said, "Tammy, I know you can't give it to me just yet, but how about I just hold it for you while you sleep?"

It was like a wave of relief washed over me, and knowing Jesus was holding it all till I woke up, I was asleep within minutes. I slept soundly that night, and awoke ready to take on the next day. That night of sleep helped me have the focus I needed to care for my son and all my other responsibilities.

This experience taught me that God can meet me where I am and can give me what I need without me knowing what it is. He is faithful. I believe Him for all sufficiency in concentration, focus, and alertness, so I may prosper and abound to every good work.

2 Corinthians 9:8 (KJV)
And God is able to make all grace abound toward you;
that ye, always having all sufficiency in all things,
may abound to every good work:

Chapter 18: All Things (Business Contacts, Open Doors, & Opportunities)

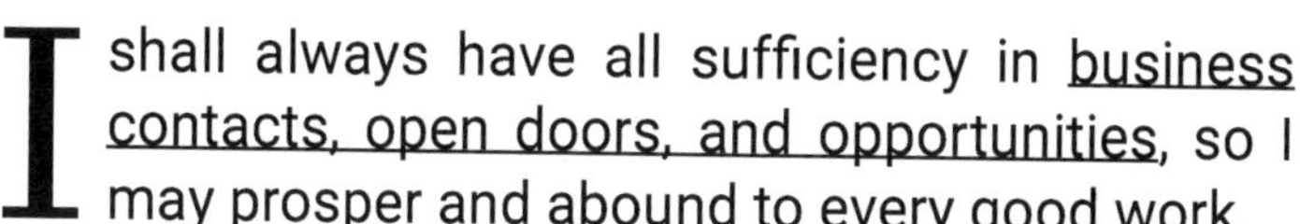

I shall always have all sufficiency in business contacts, open doors, and opportunities, so I may prosper and abound to every good work.

Psalm 1:3 (KJV)
And he shall be like a tree planted by the rivers
of water, that bringeth forth his fruit in his season;
his leaf also shall not wither;
and whatsoever he doeth shall prosper.

Genesis 39:3 (KJV)
And his master saw that the Lord was with
him, and that the Lord made all that he did to

prosper in his hand.

God blesses our hand that works, the hand that labors. It does not matter what the work is or the labor, be it physical work or laying hands on a keyboard to work; God said He will bless it.

The favor of God flows over His believers. I come to God and I speak this over my life, believing that God's favor will bring me the right business contacts, open the right doors, and bring to me the right opportunities, so my work can prosper and allow me to abound to every good work. God said He will abound towards you, or move favor in your direction.

Both Matthew and Luke share this.

Matthew 7:7-8 (KJV)
Ask, and it shall be given you; seek, and ye shall find; knock, and it shall be opened unto you: For every one that asketh receiveth; and he that seeketh findeth; and to him that knocketh it shall be opened.

Luke 11:9 (KJV)
And I say unto you, Ask, and it shall be given you; seek, and ye shall find; knock, and it shall be opened unto you.

As a business owner, I want to rely on God for the right contacts, the right doors to open, and for the right opportunities to come to me. These are all good things to ask God for. God wants to be a part of all your life. This includes your work life. We are not to just keep God in our personal lives; rather we should include Him in all areas of our life. People spend forty to sixty hours a week on their work. That is a huge chunk of time to exclude God from. You may not think you are excluding Him by not including Him but that is essentially what you are doing.

So let the Lord open the right doors for your profession, let Him bring the right contacts to help your business grow, and believe Him for the amazing opportunities He wants to present to you. He wants you to prosper above all things so you can abound to the good works He calls you to do.

2 Corinthians 9:8 (KJV)
And God is able to make all grace abound toward you;
that ye, always having all sufficiency in all things,
may abound to every good work:

Chapter 19: Understand What a Good Work is

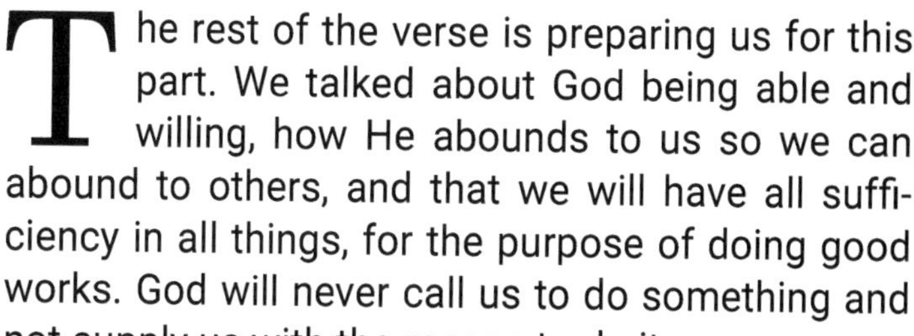

The rest of the verse is preparing us for this part. We talked about God being able and willing, how He abounds to us so we can abound to others, and that we will have all sufficiency in all things, for the purpose of doing good works. God will never call us to do something and not supply us with the means to do it.

God used the phrase *good work*, not the word *needs*. A good work is our charity work, something we do in response to a need. There is no way we can always give to all needs as the world is always in need of things. But we can always give to every good work because God calls us to *that* work. I'm called for certain good works and God calls you to other good works. If I just focus on what God has called me to do, I will be able.

When do we do good works? When God calls us to do them. This calling can be a sudden urge inside, a prodding by God, or God simply spells it out telling us to give to a good work. When God instructs you to give, trust that He will always supply you with the means to do so. And, of course He is willing and able to supply you, because He has called you to do it.

I was at a turning point in understanding giving and abounding to every good work. I had a client who God told me He wanted me to bless. This was a client leaving to be deployed to Afghanistan within five days. If I gave my client all the image files he wanted, then it would void any add-on sales from relatives from this wedding. The image files he was asking for was not part of the contract.

I was counting on those extra sales as home repair bills had maxed out my credit card and my car had been towed to the repair shop the previous week. The only extra money I had in my account to pay to fix my car was the money set aside for my monthly tithe to my church.

I remember the conversation well with God: "Lord, if I bless him I will not have my tithe to give to my local church, because the money from the add-on sales was how I would replace my tithe used to get my car drivable."

God just kept repeating He wanted me to bless my client and tell him how much He loves him. Of course, I would be obedient and do what God told me, but it raised many questions on giving and tithing.

Sometimes God directs our giving where He wants it. He had a message that day for that young man going away that He loves him and wanted to bless him through me. The joy that came from that was beautiful. It felt amazing to bless someone with a direct message from God. After all, it is all God's money and allowing Him to direct me in where I give is allowing good works to flow through me.

Ephesians 2:10 (CSB)

For we are his workmanship, created in Christ Jesus for good works, which God prepared ahead of time for us to do.

The dreams and purpose God has placed within my heart is also a good work. Doing this cost money and God knows that. We often think good works is only giving to others, providing for the poor, and spreading the gospel. But providing for our dreams and the purpose that God has placed in us is also a good work.

God may call you to travel to speak to people in an area needing help. That is a good work and there are traveling expenses that go along with it. I am called to write these books, and there are also costs associated with that good work.

I remember feeling frustrated early on when writing this book. At this point in my life I am still struggling financially as a single mom. I knew God wanted me to write this book as He had given me the book title a year before He told me to write it. In my mind I thought the job of writing this would come many years later after I had overcome my financial struggles and arrived at some level of success.

However, God's timing is not our own. I was writing my second book *The Dream Lures* in my young adult book series *The Land of Good Dreams*. In my mind I would complete the seven books and then move on to write several others including this one. But one day during a conversation with the Lord and speaking 2 Corinthians 9:8 over my life, God interrupted me. Yes, He does that. He said, "That is the book I want you to write."

His words stunned me and I responded, "Now?" As if God was not aware of my tight schedule. He responded with, "Yes, now."

Maybe others would respond, "Yes, Lord," and go do it, but I tend to ask for clarification with God so I know I understood correctly. So I said to God, "But I have this other book, *The Dream Lures*, due by spring." I had a release date scheduled with the book cover models, and yes God knew this. He also knew the stress and struggling with writing I had been going through. I could write the facts of the scenes but they lacked the emotion needed. So God said to me, "Write this book and the fire will come back to you to complete book two."

God was asking me to do something that in my mind was not logical, at least from my vantage point. I did not feel this was the time in my life to write such a book. However, God did. He said, "You have all you need." What He meant was, I already had the whole book in study notes, and He was right. So being obedient, I set out to write this book.

I had copied most of my notes over from my phone onto my computer and outlined the chapters. But I still felt I was inadequate to write this. The problem was that in my mind this was to be a success book. I envisioned a book where I showed my struggle, trusted God, and had this successful testimony to share that would inspire readers that they could do the same.

I brought my frustrations and concerns to the Lord. It was a few weeks into writing the book when I was doing laundry and I had this self-doubt wash over me. I told Him I was not sure I was at the point to be able to write this book. I asked God how I was to do it. God is so gentle and kind when He speaks to me, and this is what He said: "Tammy, this is not a book about prosperity. This is a book about believing in Me to equip you to do the good works I have called you to do."

Hearing His words lifted off this tremendous weight and pressure I had placed on myself. It was a beautiful revelation He gave me that day. When I received it into my heart, encouragement replaced doubt. Then God spoke again: "You are able."

I smiled at His humor and choice of words. God was telling me I was able to write the book *God is Able*. But the more I thought about His choice of words the more I felt inspired. God said I was able. If God is for me then who can be against me? God can see things inside of us that we struggle to see. God has a completely different perspective on my life. He is up high looking over my life and all the other pieces that compose it, such as people, places, and time. I see my life from the inside outward. I have a limited viewpoint, but God does not.

God encouraged me to write this book, believing enough in me that I can encourage others in the Lord. I think that is special. He loves me and if God believes in me, then who am I to disagree with Him?

In closing, let's take a look at what Jesus explained a life of good works looks like.

John 14:12 (KJV)

Verily, verily, I say unto you, He that believeth on me, the works that I do shall he do also; and greater works than these shall he do; because I go unto my Father.

Isn't that amazing? When we believe in Him, we are able to do those works He did and greater works, because He went to the Father and sent us the Holy Spirit.

Jesus is saying, "Look at my life and the works I have done; these were good." He healed the sick, raised the dead, calmed a storm, walked on water, and miraculously fed thousands of people.

So believe in Him and believe in God, that He is able to abide in you to equip you to do all the good works He calls you to do. The best is yet to come.

If this book blessed you, please take a moment to write a review. Sharing your thoughts with others greatly helps this book get into the hands of new readers.

Thank you.

A Bible study workbook for this book will be out soon. It is perfect for small church groups who want to read and discuss the book on a deeper level.

Other titles by T. S. Thompson

Hope Holds You

The Land of Good Dreams Young Adult Book Series

#1 *The Land of Good Dreams*

#2 *The Dream Lures* (coming soon)

Photo by Master Photographer Jill A. Bochicchio

Author T. S. Thompson is the mother of two sons currently living in Pennsylvania. She has a deep desire to move readers with her books and share the light of God through them. Thompson has been blessed with the gift of storytelling and believes the world is in need of good family-friendly books everyone can enjoy.

Connect with T. S. Thompson

www.ts-thompson.com

Follow T. S. Thompson

www.facebook.com/T.S.Thompson.Author

Made in the
USA
Middletown, DE